YOUR
AUTHOR
BUSINESS PLAN

TAKE YOUR AUTHOR CAREER TO THE NEXT LEVEL

Joanna Penn

www.CurlUpPress.com

Contents

Introduction

You are an author.

You turn ideas into reality in the shape of a book. You turn the thoughts in your head into valuable intellectual property assets. You understand how powerful the written word can be.

This book will help you use your words to create a business plan to take your writing career to the next level — whatever that means for your situation.

* * *

I'm Joanna Penn and in 2009, I created a business plan for what became The Creative Penn Limited, a multi-six-figure company with books at its heart. I'm an award-nominated New York Times and USA Today bestselling thriller and dark fantasy author as J.F. Penn, and I also write non-fiction for authors. I'm an award-winning podcaster with two shows, *The Creative Penn* and *Books and Travel*, and an international professional speaker.

My business has multiple streams of income, including books in different formats in multiple stores, and I've sold copies in 159 countries. I also have online courses, affiliate income, podcast sponsorship and Patreon, among others.

But it wasn't always like this.

I started out with one book, no audience, and no experience in publishing or online sales and marketing. But I wrote a plan for my creative and financial future and took action on my ideas, learning the necessary skills along the way. Since then, I've continued to work toward those original goals and in 2011, I left my corporate job to become a full-time author-entrepreneur. I've never gone back and I love my creative, entrepreneurial life.

* * *

In this book, I'll guide you through the process of creating a business plan that will help you achieve your creative and financial goals.

It's relevant for fiction and non-fiction authors, as well as those who want to include other products, services, and income streams. It's also applicable whether you're just starting out or if you already have a mature author business. A plan helps at any stage of the journey.

Your business plan structure

This book follows the structure of the business plan so you can focus on each section in turn as you go through.

Part 1 covers your business summary and author brand, taking you through the process of deciding the overall direction for what you want to achieve and who you want to serve.

Part 2 goes into the production process around your writing, publishing and licensing, products and services.

Part 3 covers your marketing strategy and author ecosystem.

Part 4 goes into the financial side of your business, from mindset to revenue and costs, as well as paying yourself now and into the future.

The final chapter will give you a framework for simplifying your plan and turning it into achievable steps across a chosen timeline.

In each section, I give examples from my own business plan and there are questions for you to answer and resources that might help along the way.

You can find templates and a workbook to download and fill in and more resources at:

www.TheCreativePenn.com/yourplan

There is also a **Companion Workbook** available in print with all the questions so you can write in that if you prefer.

Importantly, this book doesn't go into detail on how to do the specific topics, for example, how to self-publish a book, or how to do content marketing. I cover that in my other Books for Authors.

If you already have my previous business book, *Business for Authors*, this is a rewritten and updated sub-set of that material, focusing on the specifics of a plan as opposed to everything involved in running a business. This book acts as a companion as well as a more recent update to my own author journey. It will help you bring it all together into a coherent plan that you can use to take your author business into the future.

Let's get into the details.

* * *

Note: There are affiliate links within this book to products and services that I recommend and use personally. This means that I receive a small percentage of the sale at no extra cost to you, and in some cases, you may receive a discount for using my link. I only recommend products and services that I believe are great for authors, so I hope you find them useful.

What is a Business Plan?

A 'business plan' might seem like a dry, soulless document — the complete opposite to the creative words that you pour onto the page for your books. But think again.

Business is creative

Look around you. People working in some kind of business created much of what you see. Business creates jobs and meaningful work. It fuels income and enables money to flow between people. It turns ideas into reality.

If you can reframe business as creative, then you can also reframe your business plan that way. You are actively shaping your future writing career, and what could be more creative than that!

If you can articulate what you want, you can turn it into reality

You might think you know what you want to achieve and how to do that, but when you try to write it down, you may well discover that your thought process is fuzzy and you haven't quite worked out what you want to say. That happens with our books, and will likely happen with your business plan, but the very act of writing it down will help make it clearer.

You'll discover where you're being over-ambitious, or over-complicating things, or trying to do too much based on the time you have. You'll also find aspects that will challenge you and help you face the fears that are part of every creative life.

You'll also consider the reasons behind what you want. So often we plow ahead into busy tasks and getting things done without ensuring that our actions will lead us to an endpoint we want to pursue.

Writing your plan down will also help you to turn it into reality, because you will have to articulate what you want to achieve. As you go through this book, don't just answer the questions in your head. Write them down and turn your plan into words. You might be surprised by what you find.

A business plan has a high-level strategic focus

Your business plan will have a section on the books you're going to write, but it won't detail how you will actually write them. It will have a section on publishing, but it won't include the steps for how to publish a book.

Your plan should be high-level. Think of yourself physically rising high above and looking down on your author business as it is now and where you want it to be in the future. You can't see all the detail from high up, but you can see more strategically than if you're down in the weeds.

A business plan is more than a goal ... or a dream

I have a dream to see at least one of my novels turned into TV or film. This is a pretty common dream for fiction authors! A dream is something that you would love to achieve, but there are so many things out of your control that even if you do everything 'right,' it still may not happen. You can dream of being a brand name author like JK Rowling or Stephen King or Yuval Noah Harari, but there is no guarantee that you can achieve it.

A goal is something that could be achieved if you take consistent action toward it for the long term

I have a goal to become an award-winning author, recognized by my peers for the quality of my craft. At the time of writing this book, I am award-nominated. I made the final five for the International Thriller Writers Award for Best Ebook Original in 2017. I sat in the ballroom of the Grand Hyatt Hotel, New York City, on the edge of my seat as my name was read out as a finalist. I didn't win, but I keep taking steps toward this goal.

I focus on improving my craft, and I write the best thrillers I can. I work with professional editors and continue to submit my books to awards. I cannot include "Win an ITW award" on my business plan, because it is ultimately out of my control, but I can include, "Write the next thriller" or "Invest in a craft course to learn more about endings," or, "Allocate $X for editorial feedback." Of course, if I achieve the goal of award-winning author, I may well take a step closer to my dream of seeing my novel turned into a film or TV series. These steps compound over time as we improve the craft and the business.

Make sure your business plan includes practical steps toward your goals rather than dreams that are out of your control.

A business plan can be in any format

You're not going to present this to a bank manager. You're not pitching for funding and you don't need to justify anything to anybody. You don't have to share this with your significant other, your writing group or the internet. This is for you, so your business plan can be whatever you want it to be.

You can draw it with colored pens or make a collage, or you can use a spreadsheet. You can hand-write it in a journal, or you can type it into a document. You can use the downloadable template at www. TheCreativePenn.com/yourplan or you can use the Companion Workbook available in print. Whatever works for you.

A business plan is a living document

You're not going to make one business plan for the rest of your life. Whatever you think you want, it will inevitably change as your writing career progresses, the market shifts, and your life develops. Start where you are and expect it to change.

Make sure you date your plan and keep the historical versions. It's always interesting to look back and wonder, "why did I want to do that?" Inevitably, something will make sense to you at the time, but later on, you might change your mind so it's good to keep track of your reasons why.

Questions:

- What is a business plan?

- Why do you want to create one for your author business? Why will you spend time on this?

Resources:

- Download the workbook, plan template, question list, bibliography, and more resources at

  www.TheCreativePenn.com/yourplan

Part 1:
Business Summary and Brand

1.1 Company structure

This is not financial or legal advice. Please ask a lawyer or accountant about your personal situation.

This is a brief section so it shouldn't take too long, but it will help to frame the whole exercise.

If you already have a company as I do, then put the details into your plan. However, it's more likely that you don't have a company structure right now and, of course, you don't need to incorporate in order to write, publish, and earn money as an author.

You might have a day job and just be starting out; or you might be self-employed or work as a sole trader (or DBA or whatever it's called in your country) where you report your author income to the tax authorities with the rest of your earnings. Whatever your situation, add it into the plan.

You might be considering setting up a company as part of your plan, and this will differ by territory and jurisdiction, for example, a UK Limited Company or a US LLC or C Corp.

Some authors decide on a certain income threshold that will trigger setting up a company, for example,

US$50,000. Others set one up at the beginning, as I did, but there are overheads associated with setting up and running a company. I would usually suggest waiting until you're sure this is the right career for you, and you have enough money coming in to justify the cost and time involved.

* * *

I've run my author life as a company since I started publishing back in 2008, first in Australia and then in the UK. The Creative Penn Limited is a UK limited company with two directors, me and my husband, Jonathan, and I'm also the sole employee.

There are various author brands published through the company: Joanna Penn, J.F. Penn, and Penny Appleton, which is my mum's sweet romance pen-name, as I also publish her books.

The copyright for my books belongs to me personally, and I license The Creative Penn Limited to publish and sell them. If The Creative Penn Limited were to fold for some reason, the rights would revert to me to publish in a different way.

Curl Up Press is a publishing imprint under The

Creative Penn Limited and has its own logo and website, but it's not a separate company, although that might be something to consider in the future. I have also considered spinning out my J.F. Penn brand into a separate company, and again, that's something that might happen later based on licensing deals and income.

I set up Curl Up Press in 2017 when I started using Ingram Spark for wide print distribution. You can read more about how and why at www.TheCreativePenn.com/smallpress

Authors with more advanced careers will have a more developed company structure. If you can keep it simple then do so, but it's important to consider how you want to run things now and how you want to set it up in the future in order to protect your assets and optimize your financial situation.

Questions:

- What is your company structure now? What author name/s and/or imprint do you publish?

- What would you like your structure to be in the future? What will trigger action on this?

- What do you need to research so you're more confident in this area?

1.2 Business summary and big-picture goals

In this section, you will summarize your author business in a succinct way. This helps to frame the entire business plan. Some people might call this a mission statement, but you might prefer to consider it as a direction or a guiding principle.

Even though this is a short section in the plan, it's similar to a book description in that it can be the hardest part. You might need to write a lot of words before you truly articulate what you want, so give it a go and then circle back once you've completed the other sections, as your answers later may inform this part.

Before you write your business summary, you need to consider some big questions.

What is your 'why'?

Why do you want an author business, anyway?

Why is writing more than just a hobby for you? (Since no one ever does a business plan for their hobby!)

If you want to "make some money," consider the reason behind that.

Personally, my author business is about giving me the freedom to choose what I create, how I spend my time, where I live, and where I travel now and into the future. It means I am truly independent. I want income to fund my creative lifestyle now and also fund my investments for the future so I can keep on creating for the long term.

I also have a deep need to be useful, as many people do, and the non-fiction side of my business fulfills that need and helps my community.

What is your core life value?

This is a huge question but if you can articulate this, it will guide so much of what you do, in both your creative business and your life. It might also help you to understand why you might be unhappy and unsatisfied in other areas.

Examples of values include family, loyalty, faith, honesty, sustainability, and optimism. You can find lists of values online if you're struggling.

Of course, we all have multiple values, never just one. List as many as you think apply to you and then spend some time moving them up and down. **Be honest about what is the most important in your hierarchy.** It will help you to decide the direction of your business.

Freedom is my highest value, with the associated aspect of independence, and this shapes many of the decisions I make in business and also in my personal life. Before doing something, I ask, "Will this give me more freedom or less? Will this help fuel to my independence or will it leave me trapped in the future?"

You might have used this values list in creating characters if you write fiction. It's an incredibly powerful tool because values shape behavior and actions, which all have consequences. A positive value can also become a fatal flaw, and believe me, I know this well! For example, if you take freedom and independence too far, you might never collaborate or work with other people, you might never enter a long-term relationship, or ask for help if you need it.

It's obvious how this value has shaped my business plan over the last decade, but yours will probably be different. For example, a business plan based on the core value of Family might favor income streams that don't require being away from home; or a core value of Status might focus on pitching a prestigious agent or aiming for a literary prize. Only you can decide what's most important.

Who do you serve?

A business makes money by selling customers what they want to buy. This might seem obvious, but many authors don't think about readers until they have finished a book and want to market it. If you think about this upfront, it will help you with your business plan, but of course, I know from experience that my creative muse does not want to be put into a box!

If you know your target market already, brilliant! Include that in this section. If you're not quite sure, then we'll go into more detail in chapter *1.4 Comparison authors and reader avatar*, which is mainly focused on books, but the principles also apply if you're offering services, courses, or other products.

What will you say "no" to?

At the beginning of your author career, you will probably say "yes" to everything and try all kinds of creative projects and marketing techniques. That's a great way to start, especially if you're a multi-passionate creator, as I am.

But as you go through your author journey, tasks will proliferate and expand and you may find yourself overwhelmed by all the things you decided to start: Multiple series of books in different genres, different marketing channels with various audiences, and so on.

At some point, you have to start saying no. If you create boundaries with your high-level business plan, it will help you to say no to the things that aren't important for your overall life value and goals.

For example, I went down the rabbit hole of screenwriting for a few years. I've written a couple of screenplays. I've been to conferences and paid for courses. I've interviewed screenwriters on my podcast. Screenwriting is an incredible skill, and it's helped my writing craft in terms of story structure, but being a screenwriter is a completely different career and it's not something I want to focus on. When I'm tempted to work on a screenplay, I look at my "no" list and get back to writing another book.

Create your business summary

Now it's time to write a succinct summary that encapsulates your business. You might have several, for example, by author brand, as the purpose might be different. Here are mine as examples.

The Creative Penn empowers authors with the knowledge they need to choose their creative future. Books and courses by Joanna Penn, as well as *The Creative Penn Podcast,* provide information and inspiration on how to write, publish, and market books, and make a living as a writer.

J.F. Penn provides escape and entertainment for lovers of thriller and dark fantasy through books, associated media, and the *Books and Travel Podcast.*

Both summaries reflect my core value of freedom, and they include my target market as well as my main products. They also underpin my financial and creative goals.

In order to facilitate freedom and independence, my primary business goal is to create multiple-six-figure revenue streams from different aspects of the business so it's resilient against market changes. I also have a goal to win an award where peers judge my creative work, and that can only be achieved by writing more books, the heart of both brands.

I know it's a difficult task, but as with a book

description, start by writing a rough draft and hone it down until you're happy — with the knowledge that you can change it later!

Questions:

- What is your why? Why do you want an author business, anyway?

- What is your core life value? Or your top three, if you're struggling with one.

- How are you currently living this value? How could you move closer to it?

- Who do you serve? Who is your target market?

- What will you say "no" to?

- What is your business summary, by author brand if applicable?

1.3 Author brand

This is a challenging section, because author branding inevitably shifts over time as you develop your voice and confidence.

I've revisited my author brands many times over the years, particularly J.F. Penn, as I'm a multi-passionate creator and write across genres. Joanna Penn and The Creative Penn have remained pretty stable over the last decade. I've always tried to empower authors, and I have shared my journey and lessons learned along the way, but J.F. Penn continues to be a challenge!

But don't worry, you don't need to get it right once and for all. You can revisit your brand over time and change things as you go.

What is an author brand?

Your brand is a promise to the reader or listener. What will you deliver over and over again in order to meet, and hopefully exceed, their expectations?

Your brand includes the words you write and the emotional experience for the reader or listener. It also includes your book cover design, the look and feel of your website, how you portray yourself in interviews and on social media, as well as your email content.

You will end up with a brand if you publish books. The question is, are you actively controlling that brand? Is it consistent? Do you understand how you are perceived and what can you do to improve that?

Joanna Penn and TheCreativePenn.com are my non-fiction brand, and from the beginning, I've focused on empowerment, independence, and creative freedom. My books are upbeat self-help with a lot of practical information. No fluff! I keep a positive spin and upbeat tone on my podcast and social media. I talk about challenging times, but only when I have a positive and hopeful note I can share alongside this.

The logo, book covers, and website all use primary colors. Most of this branding was put together after the first three years of my business and has stayed stable since then. A graphic designer can help you with a brand manual which lists font names, color palette and numbers to identify specific colors, logo design, and other aspects that will help you keep consistency across your various assets. It can also help with licensing in the future. There's an example on the download page at

www.TheCreativePenn.com/yourplan

My fiction brand, J.F. Penn, focuses on escape and adventure. I write thrillers and dark fantasy, so the color palette is darker for my book covers and my websites at JFPenn.com and www.BooksAndTravel. page. I have a Brand Manual for my cover design in order to maintain consistency. My various series clearly have a similar design, and my author name is the same across the books.

Questions:

- What is an author brand?

- What is your author brand (by author name if that is applicable)? What is your promise to the reader? What are the feelings that are associated with it?

- What images, colors, and words currently stand out on your book covers and website?

- What can you do to make your author brand more recognizable?

- Do you have a Brand Manual? Is it time to work with a graphic designer to create one in order to maintain consistency?

Resources:

- *Creating Your Author Brand* – Kristine Kathryn Rusch

- Interview with Kristine Kathryn Rusch on Author Branding:

  www.TheCreativePenn.com/branding1

- Interview with Gail Carriger on Author Branding:

  www.TheCreativePenn.com/gail

- Brand Manual example –

  www.TheCreativePenn.com/yourplan

1.4 Comparison authors and reader avatar

You should have a broad idea of who you serve with your business, but in this section, you'll go into more detail around your comparison authors and your reader avatar.

These are useful whether you choose the traditional publishing model or go the independent route, and will help with the creative process and your marketing. If you offer other products or services, it's likely that your target market is similar.

Comparison authors

Knowing your comparison or 'comp' authors is useful for understanding where you fit into the publishing ecosystem, and for advertising and marketing. But it is also fundamental to your author brand and can help you to design and model certain elements if you haven't nailed them down yet.

I like to create a Keynote or PowerPoint deck as a visual reminder of the book covers and websites that I'm referring to, and I like to have at least twenty, some indie, some traditionally published.

Joanna Penn's books are non-fiction self-help, in the writing and publishing category. It's very clear from the cover and title what the books are about. Some comparison authors and books include David Gaughran's *Strangers to Super Fans*, writing craft books by K.M. Weiland and James Scott Bell, as well as mindset books like *Turning Pro* by Steven Pressfield. I do my primary research on Amazon. com even though I'm in the UK, and I also use Kobo and Apple to explore what other customers have bought for additional insight.

This exercise can also help you to see trends in cover design by genre and check that your books fit. When I started out publishing non-fiction, Malcolm Gladwell-style white covers with a single visual element dominated, but now the niche has shifted to more colorful covers.

It can be worth redoing book covers over time in order to reinvigorate a brand, but it can also be good to retain a recognizable brand over time. By the time we get bored with our brands, it's likely that other people are only just starting to recognize them.

When you have your comparison authors, you can make a list of the **categories and subcategories** that their books are in.

This might be obvious for non-fiction, for example, my books primarily sit in Writing Research and Publishing Guides, and Authorship, but you can often find new subcategories to consider, for example, some of my books also fit under Entrepreneurship and Small Business, Marketing, Business Life, Self-Help, and Creativity.

If you write in different genres, as I do with J.F. Penn, then you're likely to have **different comparison authors by series.** For example, my ARKANE series appeals to fans of Dan Brown, James Rollins, and Steve Berry. It's also good to include independent authors in the list as they are easier to advertise against on sites like BookBub, so mine include David Wood and Ernest Dempsey.

If you can't figure out where your book/s fit, that tells you something in itself!

I know how that feels as I've struggled with my Brooke and Daniel series, which spans crime thriller and psychological thriller. While the books have my best reviews, they're hard to market because they are so cross-genre and don't have clear comparison authors.

Different series will have different categories and subcategories.

My ARKANE thrillers fit into Action Adventure, Travel Adventure, and Conspiracy Thriller among others, whereas my Mapwalker trilogy spans Urban Fantasy, Fantasy Action Adventure, and Dark Fantasy.

If you're struggling with category research, check out Publisher Rocket, an investigative tool for finding the best categories and keywords, or the genre reports at K-lytics.

Create a reader avatar

This takes your market to a more granular level and will again differ by series.

For example, it's not enough to say that 'readers who like fantasy' will enjoy my Mapwalker trilogy. My husband is an avid fantasy reader, but he only enjoys long, epic fantasy series in the style of Tolkien. Anything less than eight books with over forty hours of audio each is not good enough, so clearly, he is not my target market!

A better description would be that readers who enjoy urban fantasy (usually shorter books with younger protagonists) + those who like cartography and maps, or read/watch National Geographic, will enjoy my Mapwalker trilogy. That's more specific and easier to market to.

Demographics can be appropriate for non-fiction marketing in some niches. For example, a book on weight loss for post-menopausal women will have a very specific market.

Personally, I prefer psychographics, which relate more to attitudes, interests, and lifestyle. Readers can have a lot in common in terms of their reading habits, even though their external lives might be quite different.

Questions:

- Who are your comparison authors and what are your comparison books? List by series and author name.

- What categories and subcategories are your books in? When was the last time you refreshed these if your books have been out for a while?

- What is your reader avatar? By author name and series, if appropriate.

Resources:

- Publisher Rocket, an investigative tool for finding the best categories and keywords:

  www.TheCreativePenn.com/rocket

- Specific genre reports at K-lytics:

  www.TheCreativePenn.com/genre

Part 2: Production

2.1 Products and/or services

In this section, you will consider the products and/ or services you offer within your business.

Start by listing out what you have currently, the things that already bring in revenue, and then add in any you want to grow as part of your business plan.

This is also where you evaluate what's working well and what might not be serving your business. You might need to make some tough decisions, but that's all part of the process and, over time, you'll naturally expand some areas and reduce others.

For example, when I started out, I did more paid speaking events while I built up my backlist of books and online audience. Now I focus more on creating scalable income streams rather than exchanging money for time.

Books

List your books. Think about series, standalones, novellas, short stories, co-writing, and if appropriate, any articles or papers. Split this out by **author**

name if you have multiple brands, or if that's something you're considering.

Formats. Ebooks, paperback, hardback, Large Print, Library editions, mass market editions, audiobooks, boxsets, workbooks, and special limited editions are just some you might consider.

Global markets. Are all your works available in every country in every format? If not, why not? If you've licensed your work to a publisher, check the contract for where you could also publish yourself. You might be leaving money on the table.

Languages. If you've licensed your work in specific languages, or produced some yourself, then list these, too.

If you're in the early stages of your author career, you could just type these into your plan as you won't have that much (yet!) but if you have a lot of books in various formats and markets with different licensing terms, then consider using an Asset Master List spreadsheet.

I've included a template in Appendix 3 as well as on the download page at

www.TheCreativePenn.com/yourplan

Sometimes, you need to look at what you have in order to see the gaps. Are you making the most of your intellectual property assets? For example, if you're a fiction author with several books in a series, it's worth considering an ebook boxset; or if you're a non-fiction author, a workbook edition can be worth creating.

Some long-term authors with a lot of books use **intellectual property tracking software**, but I've found that a spreadsheet is fine for most people.

Since this is a plan, **add in what you intend to create**.

For example, in 2020, I included *Map of the Impossible* on my business plan as the most important book to complete. As the third book in a trilogy, my readers wanted the conclusion to the story, but also, once I'd completed that, I could proceed with creating a series of audiobooks, as well as an ebook and print boxset that would expand my fiction income streams. I was also waiting for the trilogy to be complete before doing a marketing push.

If you don't know specific titles for what you intend to create, list them generically, for example, 'One full-length novel,' or 'Workbook edition,' or 'Audiobook,' etc. Focus on the books that will help you to achieve your goals and be wary of projects that seem exciting but might lead you away from what you really want.

This Book section will probably be the most significant, but my recommendation is always to consider multiple streams of income, especially if you want to be a full-time creative.

Here are some other sections that I include.

Online courses

Teaching in person and online is a common way that authors bring in additional income, so it's worth considering. I've been creating online courses since 2009 on various topics on a variety of online platforms. As things have changed in the industry, I've withdrawn some and created new iterations of others. I've turned some books into courses, and some courses into books.

This book has a companion course, and I also have one on *Turn What You Know Into An Online Course*, which might help if this is something you want to pursue. You can find them all at

www.TheCreativePenn.com/courses

Affiliate income

Affiliate income is commission on the sale of products or services that you promote for other people. It's most effective when you focus on things you personally use and recommend, as well as what is most helpful for your audience.

For example, I have tutorials on how to use software like Vellum and ProWritingAid, how to build your own website, and how to find and work with editors and book cover designers.

I include affiliate links in my books and share them on my podcast and website, as well as with my email list. These are useful resources for my community, and I receive a small percentage of the sale if people buy through my links. I only promote products and services that I happily use myself.

Podcast

I have two podcasts and *The Creative Penn Podcast* is a significant revenue stream with paid advertising, Patreon support and affiliate income, as well as being a marketing channel for my books and courses. My *Books and Travel Podcast* is in a growth phase so is in the content marketing section and not under Products in my plan.

It takes a long time to build up podcast revenue, but I have found it to be creatively and financially rewarding as well as useful to my community.

Services

This might include professional speaking, freelance writing, ghostwriting, editing, cover design, virtual assistant services, consulting, book marketing help, or any kind of work where you are paid for your time or for a finished product.

Services can be an effective way to make short-term income while you build up other streams of scalable income from your assets.

Scalable means you create something once and then you can sell it over and over again. For example, you write your book once, and then it can keep earning you money without you having to write it again, whereas if you're a freelance writer, you get paid for an article, and then you have to write another article to bring in more money.

Many authors use services to make more income, or even as a main source of revenue. For example, non-fiction authors can make more money from professional speaking fees than they do from their book sales.

I don't offer services, but I'm an affiliate for companies that do, for example, Reedsy, a marketplace for professional freelancers who work with authors. If you offer services, it can be worth applying to list with them.

Other sections

There are other sections you could add to your plan, for example, merchandise and other physical product sales. Just make sure you don't spread yourself too thin. I'm definitely a fan of multiple streams of income, but not at the expense of doing too much.

Questions:

- Have you listed your current books or completed the Asset Master List? Are you making the most of your possible streams of book income? What specific things will you do in this current plan to expand them?

- What other products and/or services do you currently offer? What will you add? What will you stop?

- What percentage of your income is time-based, and what percentage is scalable? Are you happy with how it is currently? How can you change that?

Resources:

- How to make a boxset –

  www.TheCreativePenn.com/create-boxset

- How to make a workbook edition –

  www.TheCreativePenn.com/create-workbook

- How to make Large Print editions –

  www.TheCreativePenn.com/large-print

- How to use software like Vellum or ProWritingAid, how to build your own website, or find and work with editors and book cover designers –

  www.TheCreativePenn.com/tools

- *Turn What You Know Into An Online Course.* You can find this and all my courses at

  www.TheCreativePenn.com/courses

- Asset Master List spreadsheet. In Appendix 3 and on the download page at

  www.TheCreativePenn.com/your-plan

- Reedsy, a marketplace for professional freelancers who work with authors

  www.TheCreativePenn.com/reedsy

2.2 Writing process and production schedule

If you were creating an official business plan for a potential investor, they would want to know how you intend to produce the things you sell. This is important for writers to consider because if you 'plan' to write two books this year, have you considered how you will achieve that goal?

Your writing process

The more books you have, the more money you will (usually) make. Since a business aims to make money and you're an author (or want to be), your plan will include writing more books. The number of books you intend to write per year will depend on your experience, your chosen genre/s, and also your mindset about being prolific.

Some people call me prolific because at the time of writing, I have over thirty books published under two different names. But truly prolific writers put out 8-12 books per year, in order to satisfy their audience and their creative drive. This includes traditionally published authors like Nora Roberts, who also writes as JD Robb, and independent authors like Lindsay Buroker, or hybrid authors like Kevin J Anderson.

Many new authors find this daunting, but once you understand how to write a book, it's more about honing your process and your craft, and making time to produce the words. If you're a full-time writer working forty hours a week on primarily producing books, you can get a lot done!

Even though I have a number of books under my belt, I have a lot of ideas and there are many more books I want to create, so I would love to write faster. I'm constantly looking for ways to improve my process in order to meet my business and creative goals.

But it's also important for your process to be sustainable if you want a long-term career as a writer. I've been a full-time creative for almost a decade, and many of the people I knew in the early days have left the industry. Sometimes they actively chose a different path, but many burned out trying to go too fast, too soon. My book, *The Healthy Writer*, goes into some ways you can keep your process sustainable.

In this section, list how you write currently and your decisions around what you want to focus on.

For example,

- One research trip to fill the creative well

- Allocate $X for books and courses on the writing craft

- Allocate X hours per weekday in the local cafe on first draft words or editing

- Learn how to outline and dictate the first draft of a manuscript

You could also include decisions around *what* you write here, as I find this changes over time. For example, if you decide to write to market, or write under a new pen-name, or try a different genre, then enter the reasons why. I don't write to market, but in 2020, I shifted my process to write a pitch document for the book before I start the actual writing. This document is only for me, but it helps to shape the book at the early stages and has improved my process.

Production plan

In my previous corporate job, I worked in several factories that produced physical goods of different kinds, and the production plan was a critical part of the business. In order to make things to sell, you need raw materials + machinery and/or labor + a process + time in the factory, and this will output a certain amount of product.

As an author, your raw material includes ideas, research, and imagination, your labor is thinking/writing/typing/dictating/editing, your process is how you write and edit your manuscript, and you need to allocate time to do all those things. The output is a finished book.

Your production plan can be as simple as a list of what you intend to produce. This might be words per hour. It might be words written or hours worked per day. It might be number of books per year.

Whatever you decide, it must tie into your big-picture goals and other aspects of your plan, like your revenue model, which we cover in section 4.2. For example, if you have a big-picture goal to leave your day job and become a full-time author, and you want to make six figures per year from book sales, then you can't have a production plan that says, 'Write one short story.'

Some authors with aggressive production deadlines use pre-orders to drive their writing, but you have to be confident that you can deliver on time to do this. Think about what is practical for your life and allow room for things to change, as they inevitably will.

My own production plan is usually pretty basic, for example,

- One non-fiction book under Joanna Penn — including narration of the audiobook

- One ARKANE thriller under J.F. Penn

- One other fiction project under J.F. Penn — standalone novel or short story or novella

Once you have even a basic list like this, you can plan your time across the year, for example, allocating four months per project, or one per quarter.

Questions:

- What does your writing process look like right now?

- Is it working for you? What could you do to improve it?

- Is your writing process sustainable for the long term?

- What does your production plan look like for the year ahead?

2.3 Publishing and licensing strategy

In this section, note down your publishing choices per project and what you intend to pursue for the year ahead.

Once again, you might do this differently by author brand or series, and if you're more developed in your career, it might also be by language, territory, format, etc.

Publishing choices

I publish independently for English language, all formats, and release my books in all territories at the same time. At the time of writing, I've sold books in 159 countries. I publish wide (meaning I am not exclusive to Amazon with my books) for J.F. Penn and Joanna Penn books in English. I don't like to rely on one company; I want my books to be available everywhere globally, including libraries, and I want to encourage a healthy and diverse publishing ecosystem. I also sell direct from my own website.

I use Kindle Unlimited for my non-fiction books in German and also for my Mum's Penny Appleton sweet romance that I publish for her. I choose KU for these because I don't have the capacity to market those books wide as well as my two main brands.

We all make decisions for a reason, and those reasons might change over time

Write down why you choose to publish in a certain way as well as how. If you're intending to pitch an agent or publisher, then you can enter that here. If you're traditionally published in some territories, you might decide to self-publish in others.

> For more detail on the practical steps, check out *Successful Self-Publishing: How to Self-Publish and Market Your Book*

Because I'm an independent author, I can publish on my own timeline. As long as I reserve my cover designer, editor/s, and proofreaders well in advance, I know when I can publish, so it's easy to schedule. If your plan includes submission to agents and/or publishers, you can control your submission date to them, but nothing else.

Make sure your decisions fit with your overarching goals

For example, if you have a business goal to make $20,000 this year and your publishing strategy is to find an agent and a publisher, it's quite unlikely that you can achieve both things within a short time-frame. It takes time to find an agent, usually six months to two years, and then even if you get a deal, it might be a year or two before the book is published and you are paid in full.

However, if you decide to make $20,000 and you have a backlist of books and an existing audience in a popular genre, you could self-publish several books and be reasonably sure the goal is achievable.

Licensing your rights

Rights licensing is the heart of the author business and your choices will expand over time as you build your backlist. Even if you decide to self-publish your ebook and print book in English, you might still decide to take an audiobook deal, or license foreign rights.

I have tried several times to self-publish in other languages, and although it's easy enough to manage translations and publish, it is incredibly hard to market books in a language you don't speak. Now I mainly prefer to license foreign rights. For example, my non-fiction books are available in French and I also have books in South Korea.

You can pitch agents and publishers about your foreign or subsidiary rights. My business plan includes steps to approach more publishers in other countries with my books, but I need to allocate time for this. There are some recommended books included in the Bibliography that can help you to up-skill if this is an area you want to pursue.

Retaining control of your intellectual property rights and strategic licensing can be incredibly lucrative. For example, fantasy author Brandon Sanderson works with traditional publishers for the main formats of his books, but has retained rights to some special editions. His Kickstarter for the Tenth Anniversary Leather-bound edition of *The Way of Kings* made $6.7 million in 2020.

Questions:

- How do you currently publish your books? Why did you make this choice? Is there anything you want to improve or change?

- What rights do you currently license and what might you explore going forward? What do you need to do to achieve this?

Resources:

- *Successful Self-Publishing: How to Self-Publish and Market Your Book* – Joanna Penn

- Wide for the Win Facebook Group for specific tips on publishing and marketing beyond just Amazon

- *How Authors Sell Publishing Rights: Sell your Book to Film, TV, Translation, and Other Rights Buyers* – Orna Ross and Helen Sedwick

- *Closing the Deal on Your Terms: Agents, Contracts, and Other Considerations* – Kristine Kathryn Rusch

- *Rethinking the Writing Business* – Kristine Kathryn Rusch

- *Hollywood vs the Author* – edited by Stephen Jay Schwartz

2.4 Pricing strategy

This section is not necessary if you are traditionally publishing, as you have no control over price, but if you're an independent or hybrid author, I recommend including a section on your pricing strategy.

Check the prices of other books in your chosen categories and make sure your price is appropriate. It's also important to price according to territory in multiple currencies. Don't use the automatically calculated price. Check on the other country stores and set appropriately, or it will be hard to sell in those markets.

It helps to write down your price brackets, as well as how you use free ebooks and pricing promotions, as you will probably change your mind in the future and it's good to have a record of your decisions.

Non-fiction prices

Non-fiction book prices are often much higher than fiction because they're seen as offering greater value and you can price higher even for shorter books. This is true in all formats.

My full-length non-fiction is usually around US$7.99 for an ebook and US$4.99 for shorter works. For print, I make sure the profit is around US$2 per copy on top of the cost to produce.

I have a permafree non-fiction ebook, *Successful Self-Publishing*, which provides lead generation into my other paid books and also has affiliate links that bring me income in other ways. The ebook makes me money, even though I give it away for free, and I sell a lot in print and audiobook formats as well.

I almost never discount my non-fiction books, so they are always full-price on the retail stores, but I have discount codes for readers to buy direct and I also put the books into limited-time bundles.

Fiction prices

Fiction is usually cheaper than non-fiction because readers are voracious and have so much choice. Even traditionally published ebooks are often cheaper these days.

I use Free First in Series for *Stone of Fire* because it is still effective for bringing people into my ARKANE thrillers. I also regularly use 99c/99p promotions. If you have a longer series, this kind of discounting still enables you to make money because customers buy the other books.

For ebook boxsets, I add up the price of the books if bought separately and then discount. These boxsets are often my most profitable fiction products.

Questions:

- If you have control of your pricing, what is your pricing strategy per genre and format?

- Have you adapted these by currency on the relevant stores?

- Is there anything you need to change, improve, or experiment with?

Part 3: Marketing

3.1 Strategy. Author ecosystem

You cannot publish a book and just expect it to sell. That's not the reality of life in the 2020s. There are so many millions of books and a multitude of other options through podcasts, TV, film, gaming, and music that you need to draw attention to your work somehow.

Marketing is the act of promoting your books, products, or services and although many authors resist it, **marketing is an integral part of the writing life and therefore critical for your business plan.**

There are lots of different ways to market your books and build your author platform, which I cover extensively in *How to Market a Book*, but in this section, try to rise above the detail of tactics and consider a high-level view of your author ecosystem.

What is an ecosystem and why do you need one?

An ecosystem is basically a network, and in this context, it's all the things that work together for your brand. This is sometimes called your author platform and includes all the ways that you can reach your readers.

If you build an ecosystem for your books, it will become much easier to manage marketing and sales over time because it will all work together in the background as you continue to write and increase your body of work. You can add in short-term advertising to the mix, but a robust ecosystem can underpin your career over the long-term.

My non-fiction ecosystem for Joanna Penn

The central hub is my website, TheCreativePenn. com. For more than a decade, I've created articles, videos and my podcast as marketing content which brings people to the site. 99% of the content is free and the business model is based on a percentage of those people buying something or clicking on an affiliate link at some point.

My email sign-up offer, the free Author Blueprint, provides me with a steady stream of new contacts, essential for an online business, and I have an auto-responder series leading people into more useful content. I've used this same call to action for over a decade, but I update the material every six months to ensure it remains relevant.

You can find it at

www.TheCreativePenn.com/blueprint

I have books, courses, tutorials, and tools that provide value to my community, all linked from the website and within the emails and content that I produce.

I own and control my intellectual property assets, and I pay for premium hosting, so I own and control my website. But of course, your ecosystem has to be more than just your own website. You need to take advantage of the opportunities to reach customers with your books and marketing content on other sites.

The most common examples are:

- **Publishing sites** like Amazon, Kobo, Apple, Google, Draft2Digital, Ingram Spark, Findaway Voices, and more. These sites ensure that my books are available in every format, in every country.

- **Podcasting platforms** like Apple, Google, Spotify, Amazon, and more to reach listeners

- **Video platforms** like YouTube and Facebook Live

- **Social media platforms** like Twitter, Facebook, Pinterest, Instagram, and others

- **Advertising platforms** like Facebook Ads, BookBub, and Amazon Marketing

Think of these as 'outposts,' places where you can reach customers but that you do not own or control. Over the years, these platforms have changed their terms and conditions and authors have had to adapt. For example, both Amazon and Facebook have shifted from organic reach to 'pay for play' in the last few years in terms of advertising.

These sites are part of the author ecosystem, but the goal should always be to drive people back to your main site and sign up to your email list so you can control the relationship over time.

My fiction ecosystem for J.F. Penn

The central hub is my website, www.JFPenn.com, which has pages for each of my books with links to the various stores and how to buy direct, as well as an email sign-up for my free ebook offer at www. JFPenn.com/free

I have an email autoresponder series that introduces readers to my books and after a period of time, includes an offer to be part of my Pennfriends team for Advanced Review Copies of my new books.

I include some content on the site, like videos from my research, but my main content marketing activity is my *Books and Travel Podcast,* which has a call to action for my free thriller. I use the same outposts as non-fiction, with the publishing sites being the primary focus for book sales.

Design an ecosystem for the long term

If you're just starting out, it's hard to imagine creating such an ecosystem, but if you think about it strategically early on, you can build something that will last.

If you're further into the author journey, then consider what your ecosystem looks like right now. Start with where you are and consider what you want your ecosystem to look like in five or ten years' time, and take action toward that.

Questions:

- What does your author ecosystem look like now?

- What do you currently own and control?

- If you carry on as you are for the next five years, or ten years, what will your ecosystem look like?

- What do you need to change to ensure it works for you over the long term?

Resources:

- *How to Market a Book* – Joanna Penn

3.2 Author website

If you want a long-term career as an author — and why would you be doing a business plan if you didn't? — then you have to own your hub on the internet, the place where people find you online. This means that you should at least own and control your website and your author domain name, both of which are business assets.

If your publisher owns it, what if you want to change publishers? If you use a free site, what if the company changes the rules or takes it down?

If you own and control your website, you can be independent and make career choices without worrying about what might happen to your online presence.

Website setup doesn't have to be expensive or difficult

Back in 2008, I had never built a website and knew nothing about what it might entail. However, I did not want to spend thousands on a design and I didn't want to pay every time I needed an update.

I spent a few weeks learning WordPress and since

then, I've used standard software, premium themes, and premium hosting to manage multiple websites. That initial investment has saved me a lot of time and money over the years, and these days, it's even easier to build and maintain your own site. It's also empowering, because you can learn and apply a skill that you will use across your whole career.

There are lots of online tutorials and options for website design and hosting. Do your research and find what works best for you.

You can find my tutorial on website hosting, design and email setup at

www.TheCreativePenn.com/authorwebsite

What is the purpose of your website?

Many authors set up a website for their first book, but trust me, if you write one book, it's likely that you will write another book, then maybe another and another! It's much more effective to have a website for your author name, or a brand that encompasses your books and other projects.

Think about the purpose your website will serve in your business and the audience you're trying to reach. Things will inevitably change over time, so wherever you are on your author journey, assess what you currently have and whether it's working for you.

Here's how my websites have changed over time

My first book was *How to Enjoy Your Job Or Find a New One,* so I set up a website with the name of the book and started blogging for my target market of miserable cubicle slaves. But I quickly ran out of ideas and found that I wasn't interested in that niche.

I set up a couple more sites, all now retired, before I finally settled on TheCreativePenn.com, which resonated with my desired personal brand and could encompass many books and projects. I also own JoannaPenn.com, which redirects to TheCreativePenn.com.

A few years later, I split out my fiction under J.F. Penn and set up www.JFPenn.com. It is easier to manage a website by author brand, but be wary of having too many, as they all take time to maintain.

The Creative Penn Limited is a multi-faceted business powered by content. Over the last decade, I've been blogging and podcasting to bring traffic to the site and drive different income streams. It's a hub for my personal brand, and of course I want people to find the free information useful, but the ultimate goal of the website is to provide revenue through book sales, course sales, and affiliate links.

The website has to drive people to sign up for my Author Blueprint and/or click links to buy. I want to help people, but I also want to make money. After all, this is a business and my full-time job as well as my passion!

JFPenn.com is more of a static website with lists of my books, links to the various book sites and social media, and a limited amount of content for brand awareness, such as videos of my research trips. The goal is to get people to sign up for my free ebook at www.JFPenn.com/free

I have several other sites, each with their own purpose

BooksAndTravel.page is the hub for my *Books and Travel Podcast,* articles and images. The purpose of the site is to build my J.F. Penn brand and drive subscribers to the podcast and email list.

If you know, like, and trust someone, you are more likely to buy from them, so the intent is to provide a more personal side to my fiction brand and build an ecosystem over time so I don't have to rely on paid ads so much.

CurlUpPress.com is a publisher-facing site for managing rights licensing. It includes all the books under each author name published under my imprint, Curl Up Press.

This is where enquiries come in for rights licensing and, over time, the intent is to produce downloadable rights guides, although I never intend to publish other authors.

PennyAppleton.com is a static website with a list of books and no extra content, not even an email list sign-up. The only purpose is to showcase the brand, but the main sales page is the Amazon Author page.

To be clear, very few authors have multiple sites like this. It's certainly not necessary, so focus on your main site first. Try to keep it simple if you can!

Questions:

- Do you own and control your author website and/or author domain name? How can you improve this situation?

- What is the purpose of your website? Is it serving that purpose?

- How does your website drive revenue? Could it be more effective?

- Do you need to up-skill in this area or work with someone else?

Resources:

- My tutorial on website hosting, design, and email setup: www.TheCreativePenn.com/authorwebsite

- Mini-course on *Content Marketing for Fiction*: www.TheCreativePenn.com/learn

3.3 Email list and ARC team

If you want a long-term career as an author, owning your relationship with your readers is the best way to ensure continued sales in an ever-changing market.

If you only drive people to the retail stores to buy your book, you will never know who those readers are. But if you build an email list, you can reach them directly.

Definitions

An email list is a database of people who have specifically opted in to receive email from you on an agreed topic. There are specialist services you can use to ensure adherence to important anti-spam and data protection laws.

An ARC team is a sub-set of your main email list and consists of readers who have agreed to read your books, some of whom will leave a review online. Importantly, they are not receiving the books 'in exchange' for a review, as that is against the terms and services of the retailers, but you can offer a free copy and let the reader decide whether they want to leave a review.

As an example, I have an invitation to my fiction ARC team at www.JFPenn.com/pennfriends

An email list will drive book sales and revenue

An email list is useful however you publish. If you want a traditional publishing deal, you have evidence of your platform. If you want to go the independent route, you can reach readers with every book.

Your email list is a business asset, and it can drive immediate sales and revenue. You can send readers to a book sales page at their preferred vendor, or you can sell direct and receive money in your bank account within the hour. You can also use that list for targeting readers with Facebook Ads, as long as you include that in your Privacy Policy.

You don't have to rely on anyone else to announce that your book is available or on sale. You can just email. If a specific publisher or store disappears or changes the rules, you can still sell books, and that is the aim of an author business.

You will probably need to learn some new skills in this area, because most of us are unaccustomed to writing compelling emails. You also need time to grow your list to a size where it makes a difference to sales and revenue, but trust me, over the years, it is an asset well worth growing, and most authors say they wish they had started their email list earlier. I would not be a successful author-entrepreneur without my email list, which I've been building and maintaining since 2008.

How to set up an email list

There are various services that specialize in email lists, including MailChimp, AWeber, and others.

I use and recommend ConvertKit and my affiliate link is

www.TheCreativePenn.com/convert

Check out my tutorial on how to set up your email list, even if you don't have a website yet, at

www.TheCreativePenn.com/setup-email-list

For details on adherence to data protection rules like European GDPR and information on your Privacy Policy and Cookie Notice, check out the free webinar at

www.TheCreativePenn.com/gdprhelp

How to attract and retain readers over time

Authors will usually use a free ebook to attract sign-ups. I have my Author Blueprint for non-fiction at www.TheCreativePenn.com/blueprint and a free thriller at www.JFPenn.com/free

I include these links at the back of every book, and in my podcasts, at the bottom of blog posts, and on social media. Some authors use joint promotions within a genre. You can also use paid advertising on Facebook and other services to drive readers to join your list.

But it's not about big numbers. It's about engagement. A small list of readers who love your work can drive more sales than a huge list of readers who don't care and don't buy. It's hard to accept when your list is small, but you want people to unsubscribe if they're not interested in your books, or if they don't click to buy occasionally.

Once people are on your email list, you need to email them

Authors vary with their strategy, some emailing regularly with useful or entertaining content, and others only emailing for a new book launch.

Research what successful authors are doing in your niche and model what works. Whatever you decide, don't leave it too long between emails, because you don't want people to forget about you.

I email every few weeks, at least once a month, to both of my lists. I include pictures from my travels or my walks around Bath, and I share links to podcast episodes and books I recommend. If people know, like, and trust you, they are more likely to click and buy your books, so definitely give some insight into your life.

This might seem a lot to think about, but your email list is critical for long-term success. If you have not sorted this out yet, it could be the most important thing on your business plan other than writing your books.

Questions:

- Do you currently have an email list of readers? Do you need to set up an email list or split out different brands? Do you have an ARC team?

- What service are you using to build and maintain your list? Are you happy with it? Are you adhering to anti-spam and data protection rules? Does your Privacy Policy enable you to use your email list for advertising?

- What is your call to action? What are you offering readers right now? Do you need to change up your offer? Do you need to set up or revisit your autoresponder email sequence?

- How are you driving people to your email list so it grows over time? How could you make this more effective?

- What is your strategy for emailing in terms of frequency and what do you write about? Are you doing a good job of communicating with your readers?

- Are you maintaining your email list and keeping it active? Are you cleaning your list and weeding out unresponsive readers over time?

- Which authors in your niche are doing well with email marketing? How could you incorporate some of their best practices?

- How could you improve your communication and resulting engagement and sales?

- Do you need to up-skill around email marketing?

Resources:

- ConvertKit, the email service I use and recommend: www.TheCreativePenn.com/convert

- Tutorial on how to set up your email list with ConvertKit:

  www.TheCreativePenn.com/setup-email-list/

- Free webinar on data protection rules, privacy policy and more:

  www.TheCreativePenn.com/gdprhelp

- *Newsletter Ninja: How to Become an Author Mailing List Expert* – Tammi Labrecque

- *Rock-Solid Newsletter: How to Grow a Successful List of Devoted and Enthusiastic Readers* – Andrea Pearson

- *Do Open: How a Simple Email Newsletter Can Transform Your Business* – David Hieatt

3.4 Content marketing

Content marketing is producing something for free — video, audio, articles, or images — that will attract your target audience and (hopefully) drive them into your author ecosystem so they will sign up for your email list, buy your book, click on affiliate links, or drive sales of products and/or services.

Only a proportion of people who consume your free content will sign up or buy something, but the idea is to get enough people into the top of the funnel so that some end up spending money.

It is *not* content for content's sake. You should have a purpose for every piece you create. There's no point in throwing something out there into the vast array of other content on the internet unless it is specifically crafted to bring people to your work.

Of course, you might write a blog for creative expression, or make videos because you enjoy the process — but this is a business plan, so take an honest look at what content will serve your business and what is just taking up time and energy.

Why is content marketing so effective?

I love content marketing and I've built a multi-six-figure business off the back of blogging and podcasting over the last decade. I enjoy the creation process and the craft of making new things in the world, and I consider my podcasts to be part of my body of work alongside my books.

It's also attraction marketing, offering something useful, entertaining, or inspirational, effectively giving someone a gift and providing value. You don't have to push, push, push, or blast "buy my book" into the ether. You can put your content out there and people come to you.

No interruption.

No ads.

No hard sell.

Just quiet attraction, which as an introvert, suits my personality down to the ground.

It can also generate income. For example, *The Creative Penn Podcast* is content marketing for my books and courses, but it also brings in advertising revenue and Patreon subscriptions. My video tutorials on YouTube are content marketing for my books, but they also bring in affiliate revenue.

What kinds of content marketing work for authors, in particular?

Content marketing is easy for non-fiction authors as you can offer articles, video, audio, and images that relate to your niche on your own site and also as a guest on others.

As Joanna Penn, I wrote blog posts for many years on topics related to writing, publishing, and book marketing on my own and other sites. Now I focus on my weekly podcast as my main content marketing tool, as well as occasional YouTube videos, and interviews on other shows. I'm always open to podcast interviews on established shows if you'd like to pitch me!

For fiction authors, your main content is your written work. Many authors give away an ebook, short story, or novella as part of their email list sign-up. Some also give away free audio or feature free fiction on their websites or on promotional sites as part of multi-author giveaways.

Many also use permanently free First in Series: For example, *Stone of Fire* has been free on all ebook platforms for years now and continues to bring new readers into my ARKANE thriller series.

You can also create multi-media content, for example, BookTubers have YouTube channels about books and reading. I have my *Books and Travel Podcast*, where I interview authors about the places behind their stories, and share the travels that inspire my books.

There are many more options for content marketing, but it's important to define your audience and create content that will specifically resonate with them. **You need a content creation plan and enough time to prepare, produce, and market your material.**

You also need to sustain creation for the long term, as content marketing is not about short-term sales. It's about long-term brand-building and enables your audience to get to know you over time. It's about bringing people back into your author eco-system and, ultimately, driving revenue for your business.

Content creation can be creatively and financially rewarding — if you are clear about what you want to achieve, and commit for the long term. But it can also be a tremendous waste of time, and you'd be better off writing more books. Only you can decide what's best for you.

Questions:

- What content marketing do you currently produce on your site or others?

- What is the point of your content? How does it attract your target market? How does it feed into your author ecosystem? How does it drive revenue?

- What would make it more effective? Is there anything you need to stop doing?

- What kind of content marketing do you enjoy consuming and creating? What suits you and your audience? What can you sustain for the long term?

Resources:

- *Content Marketing for Fiction* – course by Joanna Penn

www.TheCreativePenn.com/courses

- *Master Content Marketing: A Simple Strategy To Cure The Blank Page Blues and Attract a Profitable Audience* – Pamela Wilson

- *Master Content Strategy: How to Maximise your Reach and Boost your Bottom Line Every Time You Hit Publish* – Pamela Wilson

- *Content 10X: More Content, Less Time, Maximum Results* – Amy Woods

3.5 Paid advertising

Paid advertising is one of the most effective ways to reach readers. It is specifically targeted and can result in fast and measurable sales — but only if you know what you're doing. Otherwise, you may end up out of pocket with no book sales to show for it.

You need paid advertising on your business plan, even if you just write a sentence about why you're not going to do it (yet), or how you're going to learn the skill, or your desire to outsource. If you've already started with paid ads, then assess what's working and how you want to improve each area.

Different types of ads work for different books in different genres, so it's worth trying out varied approaches over time if you have a budget. Paid ads can be unforgiving and the learning process can be painful, but it can also make the difference between no sales at all and a viable business.

Paid email list sites

These services email readers every day with special deals on ebooks and/or audiobooks. When you use these services, you're not buying an email list and you don't get details of readers. But they usually result in a spike of sales and/or downloads over a short time-frame and bring new readers into your ecosystem. Examples include BookBub Featured Deals, FreeBooksy, BargainBooksy, Fussy Librarian, and more.

These services are most effective if you have a free or discounted ebook and/or audiobook, and you have enough good reviews. The bigger the email list, the more expensive the promotion will be. I use sites like these at least once a month for my fiction, in particular.

Pay Per Click (PPC) ads

In simple terms, you create an ad for a specific target audience and bid a certain amount for a click or impression (when the ad is shown to someone). If your bid wins, your ad will be displayed to your target market and (hopefully) they will click on it and buy your book. Authors most commonly use Amazon Advertising, Facebook Advertising, and BookBub Advertising.

There are different tactics for each site, and no one can tell you exactly what will work for your books. You need to learn and test, or pay someone to do it for you. Since the profit margins on book sales are so low, these kinds of paid ads work best if you have a large backlist with a clear target market.

Test and find what works for your books — and your happiness

I've tried different kinds of ads and ad platforms over the years and settled on a few things that work consistently for me (at the time of writing). It varies per niche and also by series and ad platform.

For Joanna Penn, I use Amazon Ads for my non-fiction books in English and German. These are mainly auto-ads which work well and need limited monitoring. I set a budget and make sure the revenue exceeds the costs each month. These auto-ads work because the genre is so clearly defined and the books have a history of sales so the algorithm can tell who to show the ads to. It's very easy — but these auto-ads don't work for my fiction at all! I also create Facebook Ads for book launches, and as part of my business plan, I'm intending to outsource some non-fiction advertising to expand my reach and sales.

For J.F. Penn, I use BookBub Ads on my permafree First in Series, as well as Featured Deals, Bargain-Booksy, and other paid email blasts to promote discounted ebooks. I also create Facebook Ads for book launches.

For Penny Appleton, I use Kindle Unlimited free days and the occasional FreeBooksy, as well as Amazon auto-ads on the Large Print editions.

If this sounds like a nightmare, don't worry!

Go back to section *1.2 Business summary and big-picture goals* and revisit why you're doing this, anyway.

My author business is about giving me "the freedom to choose what I create and how I spend my time." I was able to 10x my J.F. Penn fiction revenue with Amazon Ads in early 2020, but I hated spending time on it and resented every minute, so I stopped.

The revenue dropped, but life is too short to do things that make you miserable. I'd go back to my day job if I wanted to do that! So although I use paid ads, I spend very little time monitoring them. You have to decide what works for you.

Plan and keep track of promotions

If you love spreadsheets, you're all set! But if you're like me and data analytics is not your thing, you could use something as simple as a page-per-month calendar so you can at least see what's coming up.

I use printed pages from www.calendarpedia.co.uk to plan out my promotions so I know what's coming and when I need to change prices or schedule ad campaigns. I can also see if the calendar is empty, which prompts me to book promotions or schedule ads. It has to be a sustainable process.

Questions:

- How are you using paid advertising at the moment? What has worked well before and what has been less effective?

- Do you have a schedule for running ads? Do you track your results? How could you be more organized?

- What do you need to test or try? How could you improve your paid ads?

- How do you feel about paid ads? How will you balance happiness and sales?

Resources:

- List of free and paid promotion sites:

  Kindlepreneur.com/list-sites-promote-free-amazon-books

- *Advertising for Authors* course by Mark Dawson:

  www.TheCreativePenn.com/ads

- BookBub Insights blog: insights.bookbub.com

- *BookBub Ads Expert: A Marketing Guide to Author Discovery* – David Gaughran

- *Ads for Authors Who Hate Math* – Chris Fox

- Printable calendar pages:

  www.calendarpedia.co.uk

3.6 Social media

Social media for authors has changed over the last decade, so even if you've been using the various sites for a while, it might be time to reconsider your business strategy.

You might already use some sites for fun and personal reasons, but this is a business plan, so you need to consider how your social media usage plays a part in driving revenue or brand-building. If it does neither of these things, is it worth the time?

My primary goal for social media is to **bring people back to my author ecosystem.** It's also a chance to share more personal aspects so that people get to know, like, and trust me, and hopefully, over time, buy from me.

My main non-fiction social media account is Twitter.com/thecreativepenn. I share useful information for writers with a balance of other people's content as well as my own. I also have a page at Facebook.com/thecreativepenn which I mainly use for advertising.

For fiction, I use Instagram.com/jfpennauthor and also Facebook.com/jfpennauthor for sharing images and advertising. I also use Pinterest to create a board of images per book as I write at www.pinterest.com/jfpenn.

I have profiles on various other sites, but those are my main active accounts. I schedule content with Buffer.com, which means I don't have to be on the various services in order to seem active. I spend about thirty minutes a day on social media as part of my business, and I rarely use it for personal reasons.

Which social media sites are truly effective for your author business?

You will need to decide which social media services are best for reaching your readers, and also what works for your own enjoyment and time constraints. For example, TikTok and LinkedIn reach very different audiences, and while having a Facebook Group might be a great way to reach your readers, it won't work if you hate chatting online.

I found Twitter incredibly useful in my early years of being an author to build a network of other writers. I joined in 2008 and I've built an organic following over years. But networks rise and fall (remember Myspace?!) and they also change the rules, so don't depend on them for the long term.

Always drive people back to your own author eco-system and email list, because you don't know what will be around in the years to come.

Questions:

- What social media accounts do you currently have and how are you using them specifically for your author business?

- How much time and money are you spending on social media, and is it worth it for your business goals?

- Do you enjoy your social media time? If not, do you really need to continue? How could you make it more sustainable? For example, consider scheduling software.

Resources:

- Buffer.com for social media scheduling

3.7 Author network

A professional network is important for your author career so it's good to have a space to reflect on what you could do to improve it in your business plan.

When you're just starting out, a network is great for finding author friends who understand the roller-coaster of being a writer, as well as sharing tips for what you learn along the way. As you progress, your network will be more about sharing the ups and downs of the journey and supporting each other during the publishing and marketing process, as well as the inevitable mindset issues of self-doubt and imposter syndrome.

A network can bring you friendship, but it can also provide career advancement, so definitely make time to get to know people in your genre. You can do this through conferences, whether online or in person, and I recommend going to the same conferences year after year as a way to become part of the community. You can also join genre or author-specific organizations, or groups related to your specific expertise and experience.

I'm an active Member of ITW (International Thriller Writers), and I attend Thrillerfest every few years in New York City. I also go to CrimeFest here in the UK and I'm a Member of the Horror Writers Association and The Society of Authors. I'm also an active Member and Advisor to the Alliance of Independent Authors, and I go to London Book Fair every year where I meet other members and attend publishing events.

Networking is a long-term game

You don't just become part of a group for what you can get out of it. You have to be an active part of the community and give back where you can, whether that's volunteering to help judge prizes or manage events, as well as creating content that might help other members.

It can take a while to find the right community, but once you do, it will be worthwhile.

Questions:

- Do you have an author network already? Is it giving you everything you need?

- How could you improve your network? How could you be more active within your chosen groups?

Resources:

- *Networking for Authors: How to Make Friends, Sell More Books, and Grow a Publishing Network from Scratch* – Dan Parsons

- Interview on Networking for Authors with Dan Parsons – www.TheCreativePenn.com/networking

Part 4:
Financials

4.1 Money mindset

A business aims to make money, so if writing is your hobby, then you don't need a business plan. If you want to make money, you need to acknowledge that and plan for it, but before we get into the details, you need to examine your money mindset.

How you think and feel about money will impact your author business — and your wider life. Everyone has an emotional response to money, and you might already be uncomfortable with this chapter or you might be excited and raring to go!

The good news is that you can change your money mindset, but first, you need to acknowledge where you are now.

Here are some questions to think about in terms of your general attitude:

- What is your current relationship with money? Do you love it, want it, fear it, or something else?

- What are the words and phrases that spring to mind when you think about money, maybe from your family, the media, or friends? Are they positive or negative?

- If you're unsure, can you say out loud, "I love money!"? How does that make you feel?

- Are you in control of your current financial situation? Are you actively managing your money?

- Have you spent time learning about money? Are you comfortable talking about investments and other aspects of wealth management?

- What could you do to improve your attitude to money and your knowledge about how it works?

You also need to consider questions about money as it relates to being an author:

- Do you really want to make money from your books? Are you writing for money or another reason, for example, acceptance, status, sharing your story, or purely for creative reasons?

- How much money do you want to make from your writing in the next year? In the next five years?

- What are you willing to do to achieve this financial goal?

- What is your definition of a 'wealthy' author? Do you want to be a wealthy author?

- How do you feel about other writers who are wealthy? Check out the Forbes Richest Author List for examples.

There are no right or wrong answers to these questions, only a journey that you will experience over time. Even if you started out in a poor household with no financial knowledge and a negative view of wealth (as I did!), you can learn the skills you need to make money, keep it, and invest it for a secure financial future. You just have to want to take the next step.

Resources:

- List of recommended books and podcasts about money:

www.TheCreativePenn.com/moneybooks

4.2 Revenue model and income

*Disclaimer: **This is not financial or legal advice.** This is just my experience and opinion. Please speak to a professional in your jurisdiction about your personal situation.*

Now we've talked about mindset, let's get into the detail of your financial plan.

Use a separate bank account

On a purely practical level, you need to know exactly how much money your business makes. At a bare minimum this is Income minus Costs, which gives you a Profit or Loss per financial period, for example, a quarter or a year.

Even if you're not incorporating as a separate business entity, it's important to set up a separate bank account to manage the ins and outs of your creative business so you can track your cash flow. As management author Peter Drucker said, "what gets measured, gets managed."

You cannot expect to have a business if you're not managing your income and your expenses. It doesn't matter how many books you've sold if you run out of cash, or if you go into debt. If you actively manage your bank account and cash flow, you can be much more realistic about your author business.

Income streams

Consider your different income streams, and if you have multiple author brands, list them out separately.

You can get as granular as you like with this. For example, you might consider each book retailer as a revenue stream, or split them out even further by format. You can use the list you created as part of section *2.1 Products and/or services*, but as this is the financial section, be specific on the amount of money each makes right now and how much you want to make from it.

When you write down the amount of money generated for the last period, you will see more clearly what's working and what you need to do more of, as well as what is underperforming.

For Joanna Penn, I have income streams from book sales in ebook, print, and audio formats, from different global locations, different distributors, and also through licensing; as well as from affiliate income, podcast sponsorship, Patreon support, and the sale of online courses, plus occasional speaking fees.

For J.F. Penn, my only income stream is from book sales, although again, it is diverse and spread across formats, territories, and book retailers. By splitting this down by format and series, I can see trends. For example, ebook boxsets are my biggest revenue source on Kobo, so I should aim to do more of those.

Revenue model

This section is about considering how you drive those various income streams and how to make the engine of your revenue work.

Use your author ecosystem created in section 3.1 and expand it to include how each form of marketing feeds into your income streams. Ideally, you want every part of your ecosystem to feed your revenue somehow. **By mapping it out, you'll be able to see problems and opportunities.**

For example, my free ebook, *Successful Self-Publishing*, drives revenue through sales of the print and audiobook versions, as well as leading people into my other non-fiction books and courses, plus, it contains affiliate links. It is well worth spending money on paid ads, even though the ebook is free, as this single product drives multiple revenue streams.

For fiction, my *Books and Travel Podcast* has a call to action to my free thriller ebook, which brings people into my fiction ecosystem.

However, this is currently the weakest part of my revenue model for J.F. Penn, in that it does not make enough money to justify the time spent on it. But I know how long it takes to build up effective content marketing, so I have a three-to-five-year horizon for this to pay off in terms of effort. In the meantime, I enjoy it as a creative process anyway, and it feeds my traveler's soul, so it's well worth the time.

Evaluate your ecosystem and consider how each part drives revenue, and what you could do to improve it.

Questions:

- Do you have a separate bank account to manage your author business? Are you tracking income and expenses? Do you know whether you made a profit or a loss in the last period (quarter or year)?

- What are your different income streams right now? How much income do they bring in? What do you need to stop doing? What do you need to do more of?

- How does each part of your author ecosystem drive revenue for your business? What is working well? What could you improve? Can you justify the parts that don't make money now?

4.3 Initial investment and on-going costs

In any business, money comes in (revenue), but money also goes out (costs).

A business has to spend money, but we're lucky because being an author is one of the cheapest ways to get started.

Initial investment

At the most basic level, you only need a computer and access to the internet in order to write, publish and sell your book. You can find out how to do everything you need from online resources, podcasts, and videos, and you can use free tools and services for publishing and marketing.

But the most successful authors understand that a business requires investment. Your books are intellectual property assets, and investing in their excellence is important for a long-term profitable business.

All businesses spend money before they make money. Authors will typically spend on editors and writing craft courses before the book is finished.

They might also set up a website and take marketing courses. If self-publishing, they will hire a book cover designer and use formatting software, and perhaps invest in marketing services.

You will need some kind of initial investment before you see any financial return, and it's likely that you will spend more at the beginning as you learn skills and improve your business processes. You will also make mistakes and spend money on things that don't pay off later, but it will all be part of your author education.

I spent far more money on my first novel than I have done on any other book since. I hired several editors, went through three cover designs, attended courses and conferences, and paid for promotions that were a rip-off. It was expensive because I didn't know what I was doing, but I learned a lot! Now, after more than thirty books, I know what I'm doing and what is worth spending on, but we all have to learn somehow.

So while you *can* start an author business for free, I recommend setting a budget for producing your books professionally, and also for your own learning and development.

On-going costs

All businesses have on-going costs, and it's important to consider how these play into your financial plan.

In simple terms, if your costs are greater than your income, you are making a loss. That might be acceptable in the short term, but over time, your income must exceed your expenses. That's the only way to have a sustainable author career.

Some examples of on-going costs include:

- Production costs: Editing, cover design, formatting, proof copies, printed Advanced Review Copies, audiobook narration and production

- Website and internet tools: Hosting, email list service, social media scheduling

- Marketing: Paid ads, email blasts

- Training: Conferences, travel, books, courses

- Research: Books, travel, exhibitions

- Virtual assistant or other services

- Costs of doing business: Taxation, bank and online transaction fees, accounting fees, currency exchange, legal and insurance costs, office supplies

Set a budget for each of these categories and monitor the balance. Question whether the expense is necessary and how it feeds into revenue generation. Re-evaluate regularly and cancel anything you don't need, or look for services that are cheaper for the same benefits.

Beware of shiny object syndrome and be careful about signing up to monthly services where you don't see a decent return. Equally, be prepared to spend on the things that are critical for your business success.

It can be hard to know when it's the right time to spend on bigger costs like hiring a Virtual Assistant, but usually it's when you've been doing things yourself for a while and you feel overwhelmed. At that point, stop, breathe, take a step back and check whether the task really needs to be done. If not, stop doing it. If it is necessary, then look for help. More on outsourcing and other tools in *Productivity for Authors.*

Financial management software

Once your business becomes more developed, you'll need software to manage transactions, especially if you sell direct from a well-trafficked website as I do with TheCreativePenn.com. Many authors start with a spreadsheet, but if you're making significant revenue and/or working with an accountant, you will need software.

There are many options and you need to find what works best for you. Your accountant may also have a preference. I used QuickBooks for years but moved to Xero.com for their integration with bank accounts, credit cards, and PayPal, as well as them having an easy-to-use app for managing expenses and scanning receipts.

All financial software will enable you to run P&L (profit and loss) reports, and monitor your bank accounts and cash flow, as well as invoicing and expenses.

If you don't understand these terms, you will need to up-skill in at least basic financial management if you want to run a successful business. You can hire people to help you, but don't leave your money management entirely to someone else. Take some time and empower yourself with the knowledge you need to be successful.

Questions:

- What initial investment have you made, or do you need to make, in your author business?

- How will you fund this initial investment?

- What are the ongoing costs for your author business? Are all these expenses necessary? What are non-negotiable and important for your business? What do you need to reconsider?

- How are you tracking your financials? Is there a better option?

- What do you need to learn to improve your financial knowledge and management?

Resources:

- Xero.com financial management software

4.4 Paying yourself first and long-term investing

There are stages of the author journey and we are all at different points along the way. Your business plan for your first year as an author will look very different to the plan of someone who has been full time for over a decade, and there will be different financial milestones as well as creative ones.

Stage 1: Start-up mode

In the first years of your author business, the money will primarily flow out. However you publish later on, you will need to invest in your education and editing, and if you intend to self-publish, you'll also need book cover design and marketing. You will reinvest any income in growing your business — and that is completely normal. You're very unlikely to have any money to pay yourself or invest for the future.

I started writing my first book in 2006 and self-published it in 2008, when I also started my website, The Creative Penn, with the podcast following in 2009. Over the next few years, I wrote more books and built up streams of income from my website while working as an IT contractor. The day job funded my growing author business.

Stage 2: Just scraping by

If you keep writing and learning and putting your skills and knowledge into action, you will make more money than you spend, but it will start out small and (hopefully) grow over time. You may be able to make the switch to full-time creative if you want to, but you need to have a plan in place to cover your expenses, just in case.

I left my job and six-figure salary in 2011, but I took a huge pay cut in order to make more time for my creative business. We downsized, sold our house and investment property, and paid off all our debts as well as putting aside a buffer of money, just in case. My husband also had a job, so even though I made some profit in those early years, most of it went back into growing the business.

Stage 3: Stable income with steady profit

Once your income is reasonably stable, paying yourself will be an important step, especially if you want your author business to fund the rest of your life.

You need to pay yourself now for your day-to-day living, and you also want to pay yourself for the future, for example, funding a superannuation account or pension fund, depending on your jurisdiction, exactly as you would if you had a job. I never intend to retire completely, but I would like to have the choice and the security in case of sickness.

In 2015, I made six figures as an author-entrepreneur and in 2016, The Creative Penn Limited made multi-six-figures, as it has done every year since. I pay myself a salary as the sole employee, and the company also issues dividends to the directors (me and my husband, Jonathan). The company pays into my pension fund, and I also pay into investments from my personal accounts.

If you're daunted by this, don't worry. You can learn.

I don't come from a wealthy background, but over the last decade, I've read books, financial papers, blogs, and magazines, and listened to podcasts and audiobooks about money and investing. It's just another language and skill-set. If you learn and put it into practice, you can take control of your money and raise your net worth over time.

Stage 4: The wealthy author

When I started out, I didn't know any authors at all. Now I have author friends who have made seven figures in a single year. I'm not there yet, but it's encouraging to see what's possible when you produce quality work consistently for the long term, connect with readers, license your intellectual property, and step into opportunity as it arises.

At this stage, you will be actively managing your wealth, and looking for opportunities to invest in more assets. That is a very different business plan and something to aim for!

Wherever you are, make a plan and stick with it

If you're not paying yourself or investing yet, then decide the threshold at which you will start with even a small amount. Increase it over time as your profits rise, and put money away for the inevitable tough years as well as your future.

Questions:

- Where are you on the stages of the author financial journey?

- How can you move to the next stage? How can you increase your income?

- Are you paying yourself a salary? Are you currently investing? How can you start or increase both of these?

- How confident are you with these financial concepts? What do you need to learn in order to move to the next level?

Resources:

- Recommended books and podcasts about money –

  www.TheCreativePenn.com/moneybooks

Your Next Steps

A business plan is not an end in itself. It's a stepping-off point for the next stage of your author journey, and it's important to make sure you have a clear direction.

If you've answered all the questions, you'll have a lot of material, but you're an author, so you understand the need for editing! Here's how to make a coherent plan from what you have so far.

(1) Collate and review

Gather your notes, answers to the questions, and thoughts. Perhaps you've put them into the template or used the printed workbook, or perhaps it's in journals or written notes. Collate everything into one place so you can review it more easily.

I usually create one big document and then realize that it's huge and unwieldy and way too ambitious for one plan. You might be in a similar situation! I print out the entire document and scribble on the pages or make diagrams in my journal as I read through and try to make sense of what I've created. I always edit on paper for my books, so it makes sense to do it for my business plan.

You might find that some sections don't fit with others or that through the process of creation, you've changed your mind about what you want to achieve. You might find things that make you uncomfortable or unhappy to consider. You might find gaps in your knowledge or discover a need to learn more. Only you can decide what is critical to your overarching goals and then update your plan accordingly.

(2) Simplify

Take a copy of your document so you retain the rich information in the first version — then take a deep breath. It's time to simplify!

I'm absolutely guilty of trying to do too much, but over the years, I've learned that the best way forward is to simplify the plan, and you can do this in several steps.

Firstly, your plan should be strategic, so if you have too much information on *how* you will do something, remove it and leave only the high-level direction.

For example, if you intend to publish Large Print editions, just write that single line without specifying platforms, font size, or details of cover design. You might also have answered some questions emotionally, so remove the detail so your Business Plan remains business-like.

Next, create a new document for a detailed To Do list, or use an Appendix to separate out your action items.

Then simplify each section. If you have ten things listed, pick the top three and move the rest into a section for the longer term to revisit later. As much as you might want to, you cannot achieve everything at once.

(3) Turn your plan into a timeline

You might include some longer-term big-picture goals in your plan, for example, I want to write 50 books by the time I'm 50 in 2025. I also have a specific figure I'm aiming for in terms of investments by the time I'm 60, but the business plan is for a shorter time-frame, for example, a year.

In order to turn it into reality, you need to anchor your plan into a time-frame.

Start with a rough plan for the year and add in your focus for each month or quarter, for example, 'Write the first draft of the next book.' I like to use printable calendar months from Calendarpedia as I can write on them and then reprint them as things change (which they often do!)

This high-level planning will help you to see where you're being too ambitious and what you need to cut back even further. For example, if you've never written a novel before, you can't plan to write four next year. You just don't have the skills to do that yet. However, someone who has written several already and has nailed down their creative process might well be able to achieve that.

If you want to get even more granular, schedule time in your calendar for specific tasks. Or just assign time blocks to keep it simple, which is what I do.

Morning blocks are for creation, and afternoon blocks are for marketing and business. When I had a day job, those blocks were shorter — an hour before work and a couple of hours in the evening instead of the whole day — but the principle has remained the same since

I went full time. I go into more detail in *Productivity for Authors: Find Time to Write, Organize your Author Life, and Decide What Really Matters.*

(4) Set a review date

You're not creating a business plan for the rest of your life, so put an appointment in your calendar to review it in six months' time and see whether you need to get back on track or change it up. This is time to work *on* your business from a view high above, rather than in the weeds of the detail. Think strategically about your long-term focus, not just about the minutiae of the day-to-day.

When you want to update your plan, take a copy and add a new date, so you always have your old versions if you want to revisit decisions. You will inevitably change direction and that's absolutely fine, as long as you understand why you're making that decision.

Questions:

- Have you collated and reviewed the relevant material?

- Have you simplified your plan as much as possible to ensure it is strategic? Have you created a separate To Do list or Action Plan with more detailed items?

- Have you turned your plan into a timeline and mapped out when you will do the work that's needed?

- Have you set a review date on your calendar to revisit and update your plan?

Resources:

- *Productivity for Authors: Find Time to Write, Organize your Author Life, and Decide What Really Matters* – Joanna Penn

- Download the workbook, plan template, question list, bibliography, and more resources at

  www.TheCreativePenn.com/yourplan

- Printable calendar pages:

  www.calendarpedia.co.uk

Example Business Plans

Now we've been through all the sections, here are two finished example business plans representing different stages of the author journey. Since I have included details of my advanced business within the book, I've focused this section firstly on a new fiction author and secondly on a more developed non-fiction business.

I have not included answers to the deeper questions, just the basic plan and a few action points so you can see how the process might work for your situation.

As you will see, your final Business Plan may end up as a simple summary, but the thought process involved in getting to simple is often a journey in itself!

* * *

Example 1: A.N.Author

PART 1: BUSINESS SUMMARY

Company Structure: Not necessary at the moment.

Business (or author) summary: A.N. Author writes epic fantasy novels.

Business goal/s: Make US$10,000 per year profit from book sales alone in the next three years.

Author brand: A.N. Author's epic fantasy novels feature dragons. Images of dragons will be used on the covers and the author website, and the color palette and theme will be imaginative and playful.

Genre/category and subcategories: Fantasy – Dragons & Mythical Creatures; Fantasy – Coming of Age; Fantasy – Epic (although this category is full of big-name traditionally published authors so it is very competitive).

Comparison authors: Lindsay Buroker's Agents of the Crown series

Reader avatar: People who read fantasy and in particular, have read and/or watched Game of Thrones. They also like Dungeons and Dragons, so might enjoy Stranger Things on Netflix. They like visual images, tattoos, gifts, etc., that feature dragons.

PART 2: PRODUCTION

Products: First novel in Dragon series completed and on Amazon in ebook and paperback. Second in series currently in first draft.

Although merchandise would be great fun, it's not something to pursue at this time. No other products or services and no desire to create anything other than books.

Writing process: Full-time at day job with no intention to leave. Writing process is currently 45 minutes spent dictating in the car before the kids are up three times a week.

Action Step: In order to work toward the business goal, add two more writing sessions per week and find a quiet place for editing.

Production schedule: Finish first draft of book 2 in the next six months; start drafting book 3. Three hours per week might not be enough.

Action Step: Review how I'm spending my time to find some extra hours.

Publishing and licensing strategy: One novel on Kindle Unlimited with the intention of publishing wide once there are three novels and a boxset completed.

Pricing strategy: US$4.99. Five free days per KU period

PART 3: MARKETING

Author ecosystem: Primarily centered around Amazon as the sales site. Pinterest Boards with dragon pictures.

Action Step: Allocate time for research on what aspects of marketing might work best for these books.

Author website: Currently have a free website on WordPress.com with an About page and book details. No time to expand this currently.

Email list and ARC team: Nothing currently.

Action Step: Take a tutorial and set this up so I have some readers for the next book.

Content marketing: Nothing currently. No time to expand this currently.

Paid advertising: FreeBooksy every 90 days to promote KU free days. This works well so keep doing this. Tried Amazon Ads but it was frustrating to use and there's no time to do this as well as write. Revisit next year once I have another book.

Social media: Pinterest Boards with dragon pictures. I enjoy this and it does seem to lead to clicks.

Action Step: Set up a Facebook Author Page so it's separate to my personal profile.

Author network: Nothing currently but I need this. *Action Step:* Investigate SFWA and author groups on Facebook.

PART 4: FINANCIALS

Money mindset: I know that fantasy authors can absolutely make money from their books. I intend to be one of them but I know it takes time. I've proven to myself that I can make a small amount from one book, so it must be possible to make more. I have doubts that it could ever outweigh my day job income, but since I have no intention of leaving, it doesn't matter at the moment. It's all extra.

Revenue model and income: Book sales and pages read from Amazon stores, paid monthly into bank account. Not much at the moment.

Initial investment and ongoing costs: Costs currently far outweigh any income. Not tracking this separately right now.

Action Step: Set up a separate bank account for my book income and expenses.

Paying yourself first and long-term investing: Not doing this currently. Will review at year three.

Next review date: Six months' time

* * *

Example 2: M.K. Author

PART 1: BUSINESS SUMMARY

Company Structure: Currently reporting my book and speaking income as part of my annual tax return as a sole trader.

Action Step: Find out the appropriate threshold for starting a company as incorporating will provide more efficient financials.

Business (or author) summary: M.K. Author helps mid-life professionals to transition into a new career with books, workshops, and consulting.

Business goal/s: Make US$50,000 per year profit from book sales and services (double what I currently make).

Author brand: M.K. Author offers no-nonsense and practical advice for career change. Non-fiction book covers feature large, clear text with a color palette of deeper blues for more authority. The same design elements are reflected on the website.

Genre/category and subcategories: Self-help- Personal Transformation; Happiness; Motivational; Business & Money – Career Guides

Comparison authors: Cal Newport; James Clear; Cassandra Gaisford.

Action Step: Consider how I could also appeal to fans of more inspirational speakers like Brené Brown.

Reader/customer avatar: Women over 45 whose children are not so dependent anymore, who are ready to focus more on themselves and step into their new career. They listen to podcasts like Women in the Middle: Loving Life After 50. Their guilty pleasures include Selling Sunset on Netflix.

PART 2: PRODUCTION

Products: Six career change books and one personal memoir, all in ebook and paperback (POD).

Action Step: Consider whether my memoir fits my brand. Options include changing the author name and separating it out completely, or possibly offering a class on writing a memoir since many mid-lifers are interested in this. It would also help me appeal to that more inspirational self-help market.

Action Step: Record (or outsource) audiobook editions and create workbooks.

Services: Live workshops running twice a year. In-person event turned into an online summit during the pandemic so I know it's possible.

Action Step: Turn the workshop into an evergreen course. Consider offering consulting one-on-one as a higher-priced service.

Writing process: Currently using a focused approach, blocking out several weeks with no meetings and few interruptions to complete the first draft. This is working well.

Production schedule: I don't need any more books, I need to make more of what I have. Focus on turning current assets into more streams of income in order to increase revenue.

Publishing and licensing strategy: Currently self-publishing on all ebook stores. Using KDP Print for paperbacks.

Action Step: Expand print distribution to Ingram Spark, enabling discounts for bookstores and easier bulk purchase.

Pricing strategy: US$7.99 for ebooks, no boxsets at the moment. Will need to consider if that's possible given the cap on ebook boxsets at Amazon.

PART 3: MARKETING

Author ecosystem: Main website MKAuthor.page is the hub for my books and services. LinkedIn as main social media with a Facebook Page for advertising, which I have only used for local event marketing.

Author website: Main website MKAuthor.page is the hub for my books and services.

Action Step: The author brand name is not big enough for what I want to achieve with the wider business. Consider a brand site for mid-lifers that is not my name. Keep the author name site and redirect to the Book page.

Email list and ARC team: Small email list, mainly focused on local market.

Action Step: Look at how I can build my email list to a wider market so I can sell globally.

Content marketing: Currently writing articles on my own site and guest posting on other mid-lifer sites.

Action Step: Pitch for podcast interviews on mid-life shows. Send five pitch emails per month.

Paid advertising: Currently using paid Facebook Ads for local market.

Action Step: Expand this for email list growth and also try for direct book sales.

Social media: Posting articles on LinkedIn. Facebook Business Page but not active there. Ads only.

Action Step: Make more of LinkedIn. Research the latest tools and ways to optimize my brand there.

Author network: Women's business network meetings in person in my city.

Action Step: Research online women's business groups to expand learning to global market rather than just local sales.

PART 4: FINANCIALS

Money mindset: I still have issues around self-worth and my lack of knowledge about money sometimes makes me feel stupid.

Action Step: Read financial books and learn the language.

Revenue model and income: Currently 50% revenue from book sales and 50% from live workshops.

Action Step: Make more of what I have! Expand books into audiobooks, workbooks, and possibly boxsets. Look into affiliate revenue to make more of my website, email list, and books. Look at best options for online course hosting and start with something small. I am clearly leaving so much on the table!

Initial investment and ongoing costs: Current ongoing costs include website hosting, email list service, advertising for local events.

Action Step: I don't have enough time to do everything. Research outsourcing to a virtual assistant for helping with advertising and maybe pitching podcasts. Start with ten hours a month and see if I can justify more over time.

Paying yourself first and long-term investing: Currently reinvesting all profits into the business and living off savings.

Action Step: Start paying myself a small amount every month on the same day and also investing the same amount. Start with $200 and review over time. I have to get started on this sometime. It might as well be now.

Next review date: Six months' time

* * *

These example Business Plans should give you some ideas for your own. Of course, you might have pages of other thoughts and answers to the deeper questions, but you can see how these summary sections quickly encapsulate where these authors are now and give some indication of a future direction.

Conclusion

Congratulations!

You now have a finished Author Business Plan, a tool to help you navigate the journey ahead, wherever you're starting from right now, and a way to shape your creative future.

I wish you all the best on your author journey and happy writing!

Remember, you can find templates and a downloadable workbook, as well as more resources at:

www.TheCreativePenn.com/yourplan

Need more help on your author journey?

Sign up for my *free* Author 2.0 Blueprint and email series, and receive useful information on writing, publishing, book marketing, and making a living with your writing:

www.TheCreativePenn.com/blueprint

* * *

Love podcasts? Join me every Monday for The Creative Penn Podcast where I talk about writing, publishing, book marketing and the author business. Available on your favorite podcast app.

Find the backlist episodes at:
www.TheCreativePenn.com/podcast

Appendix 1: Business Plan Template

You can download this template and all the Appendices at:

www.TheCreativePenn.com/yourplan

* * *

Date:

PART 1: BUSINESS SUMMARY

Company structure:

Business (or author) summary:

Business goal/s:

Author brand:

Genre/category and subcategories:

Comparison authors:

Reader avatar/s:

PART 2: PRODUCTION

Products:

Services:

Writing process:

Production schedule:

Publishing and licensing strategy:

Pricing strategy:

PART 3: MARKETING

Author ecosystem:

Author website:

Email list and ARC team:

Content marketing:

Paid advertising:

Social media:

Author network:

PART 4: FINANCIALS

Money mindset:

Revenue model and income:

Initial investment and ongoing costs:

Paying yourself first and long-term investing:

Next review date:

Appendix 2: List of Questions

PART 1: BUSINESS SUMMARY

- What is a business plan?

- Why do you want to create one for your author business? Why will you spend time on this?

- What is your company structure now? What author name/s and/or imprint do you publish?

- What would you like your structure to be in the future? What will trigger action on this?

- What do you need to research so you're more confident in this area?

- What is your why? Why do you want an author business, anyway?

- What is your core life value? Or your top three, if you're struggling with one.

- How are you currently living this value? How could you move closer to it?

- Who do you serve? Who is your target market?

- What will you say "no" to?

- What is your business summary, by author brand if applicable?

- What is an author brand?

- What is your author brand (by author name if that is applicable)? What is your promise to the reader? What are the feelings that are associated with it?

- What images, colors, and words currently stand out on your book covers and website?

- What can you do to make your author brand more recognizable?

- Do you have a Brand Manual? Is it time to work with a graphic designer to create one in order to maintain consistency?

- Who are your comparison authors and what are your comparison books? List by series and author name.

- What categories and subcategories are your books in? When was the last time you refreshed these if your books have been out for a while?

- What is your reader avatar? By author name and series, if appropriate.

PART 2: PRODUCTION

- Have you listed your current books or completed the Asset Master List? Are you making the most of your possible streams of book income? What specific things will you do in this current plan to expand them?

- What other products and/or services do you currently offer? What will you add? What will you stop?

- What percentage of your income is time-based, and what percentage is scalable? Are you happy with how it is currently? How can you change that?

- What does your writing process look like right now?

- Is it working for you? What could you do to improve it?

- Is your writing process sustainable for the long term?

- What does your production plan look like for the year ahead?

- How do you currently publish your books? Why did you make this choice? Is there anything you want to improve or change?

- What rights do you currently license and what might you explore going forward? What do you need to do to achieve this?

- If you have control of your pricing, what is your pricing strategy per genre and format?

- Have you adapted these by currency on the relevant stores?

- Is there anything you need to change, improve, or experiment with?

PART 3: MARKETING

- What does your author ecosystem look like now?

- What do you currently own and control?

- If you carry on as you are for the next five years, or ten years, what will your ecosystem look like?

- What do you need to change to ensure it works for you over the long term?

- Do you own and control your author website and/or author domain name? How can you improve this situation?

- What is the purpose of your website? Is it serving that purpose?

- How does your website drive revenue? Could it be more effective?

- Do you need to up-skill in this area or work with someone else?

- Do you currently have an email list of readers? Do you need to set up an email list or split out different brands? Do you have an ARC team?

- What service are you using to build and maintain your list? Are you happy with it? Are you adhering to anti-spam and data protection rules? Does your Privacy Policy enable you to use your email list for advertising?

- What is your call to action? What are you offering readers right now? Do you need to change up your offer? Do you need to set up or revisit your autoresponder email sequence?

- How are you driving people to your email list so it grows over time? How could you make this more effective?

- What is your strategy for emailing in terms of frequency and what do you write about? Are you doing a good job of communicating with your readers?

- Are you maintaining your email list and keeping it active? Are you cleaning your list and weeding out unresponsive readers over time?

- Which authors in your niche are doing well with email marketing? How could you incorporate some of their best practices?

- How could you improve your communication and resulting engagement and sales?

- Do you need to up-skill around email marketing?

- What content marketing do you currently produce on your site or others?

- What is the point of your content? How does it attract your target market? How does it feed into your author ecosystem? How does it drive revenue?

- What would make it more effective? Is there anything you need to stop doing?

- What kind of content marketing do you enjoy consuming and creating? What suits you and your audience? What can you sustain for the long term?

- How are you using paid advertising at the moment? What has worked well before and what has been less effective?

- Do you have a schedule for running ads? Do you track your results? How could you be more organized?

- What do you need to test or try? How could you improve your paid ads?

- How do you feel about paid ads? How will you balance happiness and sales?

- What social media accounts do you currently have and how are you using them specifically for your author business?

- How much time and money are you spending on social media, and is it worth it for your business goals?

- Do you enjoy your social media time? If not,

do you really need to continue? How could you make it more sustainable? For example, consider scheduling software.

- Do you have an author network already? Is it giving you everything you need?

- How could you improve your network? How could you be more active within your chosen groups?

PART 4: FINANCIALS

- What is your current relationship with money? Do you love it, want it, fear it, or something else?

- What are the words and phrases that spring to mind when you think about money, maybe from your family, the media, or friends? Are they positive or negative?

- If you're unsure, can you say out loud, "I love money!"? How does that make you feel?

- Are you in control of your current financial situation? Are you actively managing your money?

- Have you spent time learning about money?

Are you comfortable talking about investments and other aspects of wealth management?

- What could you do to improve your attitude to money and your knowledge about how it works?

- Do you really want to make money from your books? Are you writing for money or another reason, for example, acceptance, status, sharing your story, or purely for creative reasons?

- How much money do you want to make from your writing in the next year? In the next five years?

- What are you willing to do to achieve this financial goal?

- What is your definition of a 'wealthy' author? Do you want to be a wealthy author?

- How do you feel about other writers who are wealthy? Check out the Forbes Richest Author List for examples.

- Do you have a separate bank account to manage your author business? Are you tracking income and expenses? Do you know whether you made a profit or a loss in the last period (quarter or year)?

- What are your different income streams right now? How much income do they bring in? What do you need to stop doing? What do you need to do more of?

- How does each part of your author ecosystem drive revenue for your business? What is working well? What could you improve? Can you justify the parts that don't make money now?

- What initial investment have you made, or do you need to make, in your author business?

- How will you fund this initial investment?

- What are the ongoing costs for your author business? Are all these expenses necessary? What are non-negotiable and important for your business? What do you need to reconsider?

- How are you tracking your financials? Is there a better option?

- What do you need to learn to improve your financial knowledge and management?

- Where are you on the stages of the author financial journey?

- How can you move to the next stage? How can you increase your income?

- Are you paying yourself a salary? Are you currently investing? How can you start or increase both of these?

- How confident are you with these financial concepts? What do you need to learn in order to move to the next level?

YOUR NEXT STEPS

- Have you collated and reviewed the relevant material?

- Have you simplified your plan as much as possible to ensure it is strategic? Have you created a separate To Do list or Action Plan with more detailed items?

- Have you turned your plan into a timeline and mapped out when you will do the work that's needed?

- Have you set a review date on your calendar to revisit and update your plan?

Appendix 3: Asset Master List

The Asset Master List is a spreadsheet, which is impractical to embed here. The fields below are listed across the top of the spreadsheet and will expand as your career progresses.

By listing your books in a matrix, you can see which are available in each format, language, and territory as appropriate. It provides visibility of what you have currently and where you have the potential to expand.

You can download an example template and all the Appendices at www.TheCreativePenn.com/yourplan

Book title

Language

Country (Global, or by territory if you've licensed some countries)

Ebook

Paperback

Audiobook

Large Print

Hardback

Workbook

You can break out each of these by vendors if appropriate, e.g. Kindle exclusive, Apple, Kobo, Findaway Voices, Ingram Spark, etc.)

Details of licensing deals

Appendix 4: Resources

PART 1: BUSINESS SUMMARY

- *Creating Your Author Brand* – Kristine Kathryn Rusch

- Interview with Kristine Kathryn Rusch on Author Branding:

  www.TheCreativePenn.com/branding1

- Interview with Gail Carriger on Author Branding:

  www.TheCreativePenn.com/gail

- Brand Manual example –

  www.TheCreativePenn.com/yourplan

- Publisher Rocket, an investigative tool for finding the best categories and keywords:

  www.TheCreativePenn.com/rocket

- Specific genre reports at K-lytics:

  www.TheCreativePenn.com/genre

PART 2: PRODUCTION

- How to make a boxset –

  www.TheCreativePenn.com/create-boxset

- How to make a workbook edition –

  www.TheCreativePenn.com/create-workbook

- How to make Large Print editions –

  www.TheCreativePenn.com/large-print

- How to use software like Vellum or ProWritingAid, how to build your own website, or find and work with editors and book cover designers –

  www.TheCreativePenn.com/tools

- *Turn What You Know Into An Online Course.* You can find this and all my courses at

  www.TheCreativePenn.com/courses

- Reedsy, a marketplace for professional freelancers who work with authors

  www.TheCreativePenn.com/reedsy

- *Successful Self-Publishing: How to Self-Publish and Market Your Book* – Joanna Penn

- Wide for the Win Facebook Group for specific tips on publishing and marketing beyond just Amazon

- *How Authors Sell Publishing Rights: Sell your Book to Film, TV, Translation, and Other Rights Buyers* – Orna Ross and Helen Sedwick

- *Closing the Deal on Your Terms: Agents, Contracts, and Other Considerations* – Kristine Kathryn Rusch

- *Rethinking the Writing Business* – Kristine Kathryn Rusch

- *Hollywood vs the Author* – edited by Stephen Jay Schwartz

PART 3: MARKETING

- My tutorial on website hosting, design, and email setup:

  www.TheCreativePenn.com/authorwebsite

- Mini-course on *Content Marketing for Fiction*:

  www.TheCreativePenn.com/learn

- ConvertKit, the email service I use and recommend:

www.TheCreativePenn.com/convert

- Tutorial on how to set up your email list with ConvertKit:

  www.TheCreativePenn.com/setup-email-list/

- Free webinar on data protection rules, privacy policy and more:

  www.TheCreativePenn.com/gdprhelp

- *Newsletter Ninja: How to Become an Author Mailing List Expert* – Tammi Labrecque

- *Rock-Solid Newsletter: How to Grow a Successful List of Devoted and Enthusiastic Readers* – Andrea Pearson

- *Do Open: How a Simple Email Newsletter Can Transform Your Business* – David Hieatt

- *Content Marketing for Fiction* – course by Joanna Penn

  www.TheCreativePenn.com/courses

- *Master Content Marketing: A Simple Strategy To Cure The Blank Page Blues and Attract a Profitable Audience* – Pamela Wilson

- *Master Content Strategy: How to Maximise your Reach and Boost your Bottom Line Every*

Time You Hit Publish – Pamela Wilson

- *Content 10X: More Content, Less Time, Maximum Results* – Amy Woods

- List of free and paid promotion sites: Kindle-preneur.com/list-sites-promote-free-amazon-books

- *Advertising for Authors* course by Mark Dawson:

  www.TheCreativePenn.com/ads

- BookBub Insights blog: insights.bookbub.com

- *BookBub Ads Expert: A Marketing Guide to Author Discovery* – David Gaughran

- *Ads for Authors Who Hate Math* – Chris Fox

- Printable calendar pages: www.calendarpedia. co.uk

- Social media scheduling: Buffer.com

- *Networking for Authors: How to Make Friends, Sell More Books, and Grow a Publishing Network from Scratch* – Dan Parsons

- Interview on Networking for Authors with Dan Parsons –

  www.TheCreativePenn.com/networking

PART 4: FINANCIALS

- List of recommended books and podcasts about money:

  www.TheCreativePenn.com/moneybooks

- Financial management software: Xero.com

Appendix 5: Bibliography

Closing the Deal on Your Terms: Agents, Contracts, and Other Considerations – Kristine Kathryn Rusch

Content 10X: More Content, Less Time, Maximum Results – Amy Woods

Creating Your Author Brand – Kristine Kathryn Rusch

Do Open: How a Simple Email Newsletter Can Transform Your Business – David Hieatt

Hollywood vs the Author – edited by Stephen Jay Schwartz

How to Market a Book – Joanna Penn

How Authors Sell Publishing Rights: Sell your Book to Film, TV, Translation, and Other Rights Buyers – Orna Ross and Helen Sedwick

Master Content Marketing: A Simple Strategy To Cure The Blank Page Blues and Attract a Profitable Audience – Pamela Wilson

Master Content Strategy: How to Maximise your Reach and Boost your Bottom Line Every Time You Hit Publish – Pamela Wilson

Money Book List:

www.TheCreativePenn.com/moneybooks

Networking for Authors: How to Make Friends, Sell More Books, and Grow a Publishing Network from Scratch – Dan Parsons

Newsletter Ninja: How to Become an Author Mailing List Expert – Tammi Labrecque

Productivity for Authors: Find Time to Write, Organize your Author Life, and Decide What Really Matters – Joanna Penn

Rethinking the Writing Business – Kristine Kathryn Rusch

Rock-Solid Newsletter: How to Grow a Successful List of Devoted and Enthusiastic Readers – Andrea Pearson

Successful Self-Publishing: How to Self-Publish and Market Your Book – Joanna Penn

About Joanna Penn

Joanna Penn, writing as J.F.Penn, is an award-nominated, New York Times and USA Today bestselling author of thrillers and dark fantasy, as well as writing inspirational non-fiction for authors.

She is an international professional speaker, podcaster, and award-winning entrepreneur. She lives in Bath, England with her husband and enjoys a nice G&T.

Joanna's award-winning site for writers, TheCreativePenn.com, helps people to write, publish and market their books through articles, audio, video and online products as well as live workshops.

Love thrillers? www.JFPenn.com

Love travel? www.BooksAndTravel.page

Connect with Joanna
www.TheCreativePenn.com
joanna@TheCreativePenn.com

www.twitter.com/thecreativepenn
www.facebook.com/TheCreativePenn
www.Instagram.com/jfpennauthor
www.youtube.com/thecreativepenn

More Books and Courses from Joanna Penn

Non-Fiction Books for Authors

How to Write Non-Fiction

How to Market a Book

How to Make a Living with your Writing

Productivity for Authors

Successful Self-Publishing

Your Author Business Plan

The Successful Author Mindset

Public Speaking for Authors,
Creatives and Other Introverts

Audio for Authors:
Audiobooks, Podcasting, and Voice Technologies

The Healthy Writer

Business for Authors:
How to be an Author Entrepreneur

Career Change

www.TheCreativePenn.com/books

Courses for Authors

How to Write a Novel

How to Write Non-Fiction

Multiple Streams of Income from your Writing

Your Author Business Plan

Content Marketing for Fiction

Productivity for Authors

Turn What You Know Into An Online Course

Co-Writing a Book

www.TheCreativePenn.com/courses

***

Thriller and Dark Fantasy Novels as J.F.Penn

ARKANE Action-adventure Thrillers

Stone of Fire #1
Crypt of Bone #2
Ark of Blood #3
One Day in Budapest #4
Day of the Vikings #5
Gates of Hell #6
One Day in New York #7
Destroyer of Worlds #8
End of Days #9
Valley of Dry Bones #10
Tree of Life #11

Brooke and Daniel Crime Thrillers

Desecration #1
Delirium #2
Deviance #3

Mapwalker Dark Fantasy Trilogy

Map of Shadows #1
Map of Plagues #2
Map of the Impossible #3

Other books and short stories

Risen Gods

A Thousand Fiendish Angels

The Dark Queen

More books coming soon.

Get your free thriller at:
www.JFPenn.com/free

Acknowledgments

Thanks to my community at The Creative Penn and my Patreon supporters for continuing to support my writing life. When I suffer the inevitable self-doubt, you help me remember that I can still be useful by sharing my journey.

Thanks to Sacha Black and Alexandra Amor for beta reading, and to Liz Dexter at Libroediting for speedy proofreading. Thanks to Jane Dixon Smith for the cover design and print formatting.

Manufactured by Amazon.ca
Acheson, AB